Only in New York

500 Photos · 500 Moments

Only in New York

By the Photography Staff of *The New York Times*

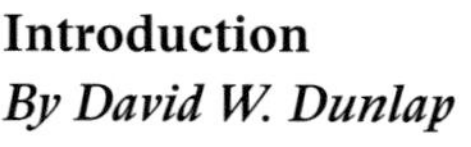

Introduction
By David W. Dunlap

David W. Dunlap was a metro reporter for The Times *from 1981 to 2017.*

You've already looked through the pictures. You understand they're meant to be seen as diptychs. But some pairings eluded you on first glance.

That's O.K. You're supposed to do more than look just once. The juxtapositions invite you to savor the photos. Spend time with them. They'll reward your close study, often with a laugh.

What, for instance, has a crated giraffe to do with the Roosevelt Island tram? *(pp. 248–249.)* Well, you might think of the theme as "The Transportation of Mammals Over Bodies of Water, Standing in Cramped Boxes Held Aloft by Slender Cables."

The glinting subway train and a couple of old-time baseball players? *(pp. 104–105.)* Zoom in a bit. That train shares a number with Mickey Mantle of the Yankees, who is standing with Yogi Berra and Casey Stengel in Shea Stadium. Which you reached on the No. 7 train.

Multiple meanings abound. Yes, the graduates of the Police Academy will soon be handing out tickets. *(pg. 86)* But a second glance reveals showers in both photos.

Colors may be just one of the facets the pictures have in common. *(pp. 44–45.)* Watch for patterns. *(pp. 26–27.)* And shapes. *(pp. 326–327.)* Form. *(pp. 48–49.)* Function *(pp. 208–209.)* Be alert for irony. *(pp. 90–91.)* And the occasional pun. *(pg. 150.)* Or a message on one page that applies equally to the other. *(pg. 372.)* *Only in New York* highlights the threads that hold this city of contrasts together.

It also celebrates the contemporary photojournalists who have made *The Times* a Pulitzer-winning leader in visual presentation. Equally important, it honors earlier generations of photographers who labored creatively and tirelessly when *The Times* had a reputation—often well deserved—for being indifferent to good photography.

Years ago, these photographers created an astonishing body of work. *The Times* may not have used it to best advantage at the time. But the company was, at least, smart enough to hang on to millions of prints, negatives, contact sheets, and computer files.

When we opened the archive and started laying out the pages for this book, we found that certain pictures had an affinity for one another—regardless of when they were taken or where or by whom. Paradoxically, each photograph came into sharper focus when set into a diptych.

Wordlessly, the pairings began telling stories of their own.

They spoke across time. They described a city that exists on many planes simultaneously: energetic and brutal, compassionate and cruel, creative and desperate, eccentric and conformist, impatient and steady, exuberant and serene, tragic and funny, elegant and shabby, cosmopolitan and insular, crowded and lonely.

New York is not always an assault on the senses. It can reveal itself subtly, too. All that's required is that you look.

And look again.

Cats at the Winter Garden Theater, 1997
Sara Krulwich

Dogs on the leash, Washington and Bank Streets, Manhattan, 2016

Nicole Bengiveno

Souvenirs, Vesey and Church Streets, Manhattan, 2016
Todd Heisler

Lady Liberty, Battery Park, 2013

Suzanne DeChillo

Underground Manhattan, 1976
Neal Boenzi

No. 1 Train, 1979
Neal Boenzi

New York City Marathon, 106th Street and Fifth Avenue, Manhattan, 2005
Vincent Laforet

New York City Marathon finishers, Central Park, 2005
Vincent Laforet

Fulton Center, Manhattan, 2014
Damon Winter

World Trade Center Transportation Hub, Manhattan, 2016
Richard Perry

Stickball world series, East Harlem, 1984
Joyce Dopkeen

Derek Jeter, Yankee Stadium, 2009
Barton Silverman

“Driving down deserted Fifth Avenue late one night,” writes Brent C. Brolin, “my wife and I were startled to see a man on the sidewalk getting ready to throw something into the entrance of the Aeroflot offices (the Russian airline). Wary of a bomb blast, we drove by cautiously on the far side of the street. As we passed the doorway we were relieved to recognize two of New York’s finest; one was pitching wadded paper bags; the other, partially hidden in the doorway, was batting them back with his billy club.”

Grand Ferry Park, Williamsburg, Brooklyn, 2008
Damon Winter

Staten Island Ferry, New York Harbor, 1979
Neal Boenzi

Flatiron Building, Manhattan, 2002
Vincent Laforet

Celebrating the Brooklyn Bridge's 125th, East River, 2008
Josh Haner

Carriages on Fifth Avenue near 32nd Street, 1917

The New York Times

City Hall Park, 1913
The New York Times

Martin Scorsese, Jersey Alley, SoHo, 1988
Sara Krulwich

Frank Sinatra, Upper East Side, 1967

Neal Boenzi

Upper West Side, 2009
Ruth Fremson

Brooklyn Bridge, from Manhattan, 2011

Librado Romero

Ornithology devotees, Central Park Ramble, 1960
Robert Walker

Civil Defense Air Raid Drill, Midtown Manhattan, 1952
Larry C. Morris

Easter Sunday, Abyssinian Baptist Church, Harlem, 2007
Ozier Muhammad

At Barneys, Midtown Manhattan, 1998
Edward Keating

Minnie the elephant, Coney Island, 2009
Ruby Washington

On the beach, Coney Island, 1975

William E. Sauro

Empire State Building, 1997
Chang W. Lee

Miss New York City Pageant, Midtown Manhattan, 2007
Richard Perry

James Lewis Jr., Coney Island, 1970
Barton Silverman

Mayor Fiorello La Guardia and family,
World's Fair, Flushing Meadows, Queens, 1939
The New York Times

Sign seen by Cy Schleifer in the window of a luncheonette on Avenue A near 11th Street:
FRANKFURTERS AVEC BEANS

Fire explosion, Broadway and 40th Street, 1957
Meyer Liebowitz

Five-alarmer, Spring and Greene Streets, 1957
Carl T. Gossett Jr.

North Fountain, 9/11 Memorial, World Trade Center complex, 2011
Damon Winter

Observation Deck, Rockefeller Center, 2010
Richard Perry

Frank Kind on the 46th Floor, 888 Seventh Avenue, 1995
Andrea Mohin

The Cloisters, Fort Tryon Park, 2002
Damon Winter

West Indies Day Parade, Brooklyn, 2001
Vincent Laforet

Chinese New Year Flower Market, Columbus Park, Chinatown, 2006
Marilynn K. Yee

Mark Pinn trims the lawn, Harlem, 2008
Todd Heisler

14th Street, 2006
Nicole Bengiveno

L.G. Khambache Sherpa prepares for a charity crawl, Brooklyn, 2005

Tyler Hicks

Spiderman on Thanksgiving Day, Central Park West, 2012
Suzanne DeChillo

Out-of-town musicians in the snow, St. Patrick's Day Parade route, 1982

Neal Boenzi

New York City Ballet dancers in *The Nutcracker*, Lincoln Center, 2011
Andrea Mohin

Crosstown bus, Manhattan, 1960
Sam Falk

Theater District, Manhattan, 2003
James Estrin

R. Chester Redhead is waiting for the No. 1 bus on 86th Street and Madison Avenue. When it finally arrives, the woman in front of Mr. Redhead hands the driver a transfer. “Lady,” he says, “this transfer is from yesterday.” “That tells you how long I’ve been waiting for this bus,” she replies.

Flushing Mall, Queens, 2006
Nicole Bengiveno

World Cup celebrants, Little Korea, Manhattan, 2006

Angel Franco

Queen Mary 2 arrives, New York Harbor, 2004
Fred R. Conrad

Space shuttle fly-by, Midtown Manhattan, 2012
Dan Neville

Jefferson Airplane fans, Great Lawn, Central Park, 1972
Don Hogan Charles

Columbia University Commencement, Manhattan, 2007
Librado Romero

Chrysler Building, Midtown Manhattan, 2003
Vincent Laforet

The Trylon and Perisphere, World's Fair, Flushing, Queens, 1939
William C. Eckenberg

125th Street, Harlem, 1975
Meyer Liebowitz

Shanghai Beauty Shop, Lower Manhattan, 1974
Neal Boenzi

Barclays Center, Brooklyn, 2012
Richard Perry

Beneath the Gould Library, Bronx Community College, 2004
Suzanne DeChillo

Standing guard at Macy's, 1955
Larry C. Morris

New York Aquarium, Coney Island, 1960
Sam Falk

Turtle Pond, Central Park, 2006
Ruth Fremson

Inwood Hill Park, Upper Manhattan, 2009
Suzanne DeChillo

The Frick Collection, Upper East Side, 2008
Librado Romero

President Barack Obama, United Nations General Assembly, 2015
Damon Winter

Dear Diary:

During the United Nations summit conference, my husband and I were looking for a taxi on Second Avenue and 45th Street for what seemed like an eternity. While waiting, we chatted with a young police officer on duty. He suggested that we walk to Third Avenue, even though my husband has to use a cane. We followed his advice and halfway down the block, I spotted a cab with its lights on and flagged it down. To our amazement, who should step out but the very same officer. He had hailed the cab and brought it around for us. Who says the police are not caring and considerate?

Barbara Kleinberg

Inside Lady Liberty's Crown, Liberty Island, 1962
Neal Boenzi

Restoring the torch, Liberty Island, 1986
Keith Meyers

Guineviere in a limo, Manhattan, 1997

Andrea Mohin

West 42nd Street, Manhattan, 2008
Chang W. Lee

Patrick Ewing and Charles Oakley scrambling, Madison Square Garden, 1993
Barton Silverman

Edson Arantes do Nascimento, aka Pele, Midtown Manhattan, West Side, 1971

Meyer Liebowitz

Westchester Corp. Tires and Wheels Center, Bronx, 2009
Nicole Bengiveno

Long Island Expressway, Queens, 2013
Barton Silverman

Westminster Kennel Club Dog Show, Madison Square Garden, 2012
Barton Silverman

Gertrude goes for a walk, Eighth Avenue, Midtown Manhattan, 1974
Neal Boenzi

Manhattan Detention Complex, White Street, 1941
The New York Times

Tudor City, East 42nd, 2010
Earl Wilson

Earl Prince, 14, Brooklyn, 1987
Fred R. Conrad

Outward Bound benefit, Plaza Hotel, 1976
Chester Higgins Jr.

Police Academy graduation, Madison Square Garden, 2006
Nicole Bengiveno

Federal Plaza, 2014
Ozier Muhammad

"Do you ever ask why rules and penalties do not work in New York City?" writes Richard Reilly. "Recently I was waiting on a street corner in midtown for an associate. During my wait, a police tow truck hooked up one of many cars illegally parked in a tow-away zone. During the operation, a frustrated driver who had given up looking for a parking place pulled up alongside the car being towed and waited. After the tow truck pulled the offending car out of its place, the waiting driver pulled up, backed into the empty space, turned off the motor, left the car and walked away.

"He had found his parking space."

Boarding a TWA Constellation, Idlewild Airport, Queens, 1954

Sam Falk

Martha Graham and dancers rehearse *Acrobats of God*, 54th Street Theatre, 1960
Sam Falk

Donald J. Trump, Midtown Manhattan, 1985
Neal Boenzi

Ellis Island, 1989
Marilynn K. Yee

The talk of Bryant Park, 2012
Damon Winter

P.S.158 sixth-graders answer the call, Upper East Side, 1975
Meyer Liebowitz

Joe Frazier and Muhammad Ali, Madison Square Garden, 1971
Larry C. Morris

Jack Dempsey greets diners at his restaurant on Broadway, 1954
Sam Falk

View from the subway entrance, Columbus Circle, 2016
Todd Heisler

Hayden Planetarium, Central Park West, 2000

Sara Krulwich

Breezy Point, Queens, 2008
Suzanne DeChillo

Hansel and Gretel, Metropolitan Opera House, 2017
Sara Krulwich

Guggenheim Museum, Upper East Side, 1998
Edward Keating

Grand Central Parkway and Van Wyck Expressway, Queens, 1955
Meyer Liebowitz

Overheard by Deborah A. Goldberg at the Guggenheim Museum during the recent *Art of the Motorcycle* exhibition: "I always thought this would make a good garage."

Chambers Street subway station, 2011
Fred R. Conrad

Exact location unknown, 1960
Sam Falk

No. 7 Train, 69th Street Station, Queens, 2010
Chang W. Lee

Mickey Mantle, Yogi Berra, and Casey Stengel, Shea Stadium, 1964
Larry C. Morris

Smith Street Tattoo Parlour, Brooklyn, 2013
Nicole Bengiveno

May's Nails Salon, West 14th Street, 2014

Nicole Bengiveno

Central Park, 2008

Todd Heisler

Brighton Beach, Brooklyn, 2014
Todd Heisler

West 47th Street, Manhattan, 1976

D. Gorton

Bronx Zoo, 1977
John Sotomayor

Ellis Island bound, New York Harbor, 2002
Edward Keating

Staten Island bound, New York Harbor, 2010
Librado Romero

The Let There Be Neon Studio, Manhattan, 2010
Ruth Fremson

Easter Parade, Fifth Avenue, 2013
Fred R. Conrad

Morris Avenue, Bronx, 2006
Richard Perry

New York University Commencement,
Yankee Stadium, 2010
Richard Perry

THE CITY'S A STAGE
where people acting in their daily lives
are more interesting than performance artists
who strive
to get our attention
by dousing their bodies with substances
I won't mention.

Ed Rossman

Oscar de la Renta show, Park Avenue, 2009

Damon Winter

Metro North out of Grand Central Terminal, Date unknown
Larry C. Morris

Mourning Benazir Bhutto, Makki Mosque, Brooklyn, 2007
Chang W. Lee

Marking the end of Ramadan, Queens, 2013
Angel Franco

Columbus Park, Chinatown, 2010

Ruth Fremson

Rescuing a turkey race competitor, Grand Street Settlement, Manhattan, 1958
Arthur Brower

USS *Akron* airship, 1931
The New York Times

Stunt pilot Sean D. Tucker on a practice run, 2007
Vincent Laforet

Tyson the carriage horse, Manhattan, 2015
Michelle V. Agins

Gene Autry and Champion go for a ride, Manhattan, 1948
William C. Eckenberg

Alberto Salazar wins the New York City Marathon, 1982
Marilynn K. Yee

Aquatic aerobics, Astoria, Queens, 2001
Ruth Fremson

Nina Simone at The Village Gate, 1965
Sam Falk

Loving what she hears, Venue unknown, 1954
Sam Falk

Masterpiece fatigue, Museum of Modern Art, 2008
Nicole Bengiveno

Yoga on the roof, Manhattan, 2005
James Estrin

Tanning at the landfill, Battery Park City, 1977
Fred R. Conrad

. . . and the F.D.R., Manhattan, 2000
James Estrin

Overheard by Harvey E. Phillips on a street in Greenwich Village, young man to his companion: "Oh, I've stopped going to the Hamptons. It's too much like going uptown."

The Garment Worker, Fashion District, Manhattan, 2012
Librado Romero

Garment factory workers, Chinatown, 1967
Arthur Brower

The 90-story One57 building, Midtown Manhattan, 2012
Chang W. Lee

Installation of a Coke sign, Duffy Square, Broadway, 2004
Fred R. Conrad

Saturday Night Fever before the movie, Regine's Disco, Manhattan, 1976
Larry C. Morris

. . . and long after, Odyssey Disco, Bay Ridge, Brooklyn, 2017
Damon Winter

Rockefeller Center, 2017
Hiroko Masuike

Park Slope, Brooklyn, 2010

Ruth Fremson

Doug Walker and the New York City Float Committee, Times Square, 2007
Damon Winter

Dance Theatre of Harlem at City Center, Manhattan, 1984
Keith Meyers

Metropolitan Museum of Art, 1976
Neal Boenzi

Sphinx of Hatshepsut, Metropolitan Museum of Art, 2015
Todd Heisler

The downtown piers, Bethune Street and the Hudson River, 1978

Paul Hosefros

Upper Manhattan, 1987

Neal Boenzi

Christopher Street, 1981
William E. Sauro

Greenwich Street, 2002
Nicole Bengiveno

CITY DOGS

City dogs
Are so polite
Seldom bite
Laugh at dangers
Sniff at strangers
Eat croissants
Love *enfants*
Marrow bones
Ice-cream cones
Feathered migrants
Fire hydrants.

PEGGY KEILUS

The New York Stock Exchange, Lower Manhattan, 2008
Todd Heisler

Times Square, 2008
Nicole Bengiveno

Central Park, 1955
Ernie Sisto

Peter J. Sharp Boathouse, East River, Manhattan, 2012
James Estrin

New York Giants' football fans watch their team from
a nearby rooftop, Bronx, 1970
Ernie Sisto

U.S. Open, Day 1, Arthur Ashe Stadium, Queens, 2009
Richard Perry

Midtown Manhattan as snow falls, 2006
Chang W. Lee

Metro North train passing through Riverdale, Bronx, 2012
Librado Romero

East River State Park, Williamsburg, Brooklyn, 2015
Damon Winter

The Gotham Book Mart, R.I.P., West 47th Street, 1997
Joyce Dopkeen

World Trade Center, 2001
Tyler Hicks

St. Charlie's bar and restaurant, Albany Street, Lower Manhattan, 2001

Tyler Hicks

Avenue of the Americas, Midtown Manhattan, 2010
Ruth Fremson

Searching for errant pigeons, Union Carbide Building, Park Avenue, 1960
Ernie Sisto

Queens Plaza Street, Queens, 2006
Richard Perry

Brooklyn MTA rail yard, Coney Island, 2005
Vincent Laforet

Dear Diary:

Riding on a crowded F train between Manhattan and Queens, I stood near a woman and her young son. As the train pulled out of the last station in Manhattan, the woman started to explain to her son that we were passing through a tunnel under the East River. When the train arrived at their first stop in Queens, she had just finished her commentary on the trip, saying, ". . . and here we are in Queens: and that's why they call us bridge and tunnel people."

SUSAN LEVEN-WEINBERG

Fifth Avenue and Washington Square Park, 1946
Ernie Sisto

Canal Street at the foot of the Manhattan Bridge, 2007
Todd Heisler

Bobby Fischer and Andrew Soltis, Manhattan Chess Club, 1971
Larry C. Morris

Ishmael Sylle, 12, Parkside Community Center, Bronx, 2008
James Estrin

Lower East Side, 1962
Meyer Liebowitz

Upper East Side, 2015

Hiroko Masuike

The Rockettes, Radio City Music Hall, 1930s
The New York Times

Opening of the new Metropolitan Opera House, Lincoln Center, 1966
Jack Manning

Annemarie de Nonno and the Giglio Band, Williamsburg, Brooklyn, 2014
Damon Winter

Stephen Colbert, Ed Sullivan Theater, 2015
Damon Winter

Demonstrating the "Bell Rocket Belt," World's Fair, Flushing, Queens, 1964
The New York Times

P.S. 121, Manhattan, 1967
Eddie Hausner

Central Park, late fall, 1997
Dith Pran

One57, North View, 2012
Chang W. Lee

MY CENTRAL PARK

If only God can make a tree
Then Central Park must be heaven
Could I but have my ashes spread
Where my feet had slowly walked
Past Strawberry Fields,
To cheers where bat meets ball
Toward laughter at the zoo
Past picnic chatter
To a bench where I had daydreamed beside cool water
Then lift me to where the Bard holds forth
Toward tennis court and path around the reservoir
Toward sweet scented air
Then settle me on the Great Lawn
Where music plays
For all eternity.

MANNY KUSSACK

Kermit passing by West 75th Street, 2007
Todd Heisler

Apple Store, Fifth Avenue and 59th Street, 2009
Nicole Bengiveno

137th Street, Bronx, 1962

Neal Boenzi

Women's Bureau, Auxiliary Police, Manhattan, 1952
Neal Boenzi

Long Island City, 2015
Hiroko Masuike

Joe and Pat's Pizzeria, Staten Island, 2013
Tony Cenicola

Yankee Stadium, 1965
Ernie Sisto

Mayor Edward I. Koch, City Hall, 1985
Neal Boenzi

Lou Reed, St. Ann's Warehouse, Brooklyn, 2006
Richard Perry

West 106th Street, Manhattan, 2014
Angel Franco

Black Panthers, Manhattan, 1969

Neal Boenzi

New York State Supreme Court, Manhattan, 2011
Hiroko Masuike

Lasker Pool, Central Park, 2006
Nicole Bengiveno

Bronx, 1999
James Estrin

Chinatown, Manhattan, 2006
Chang W. Lee

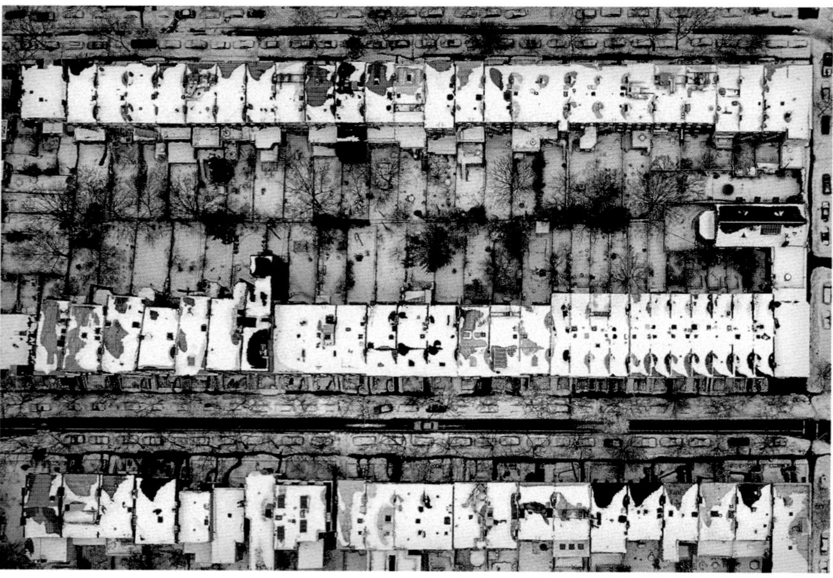

Flatbush, Brooklyn, 2003
Vincent Laforet

TAXI, TAXI

Thanks to New York cabbies
My travel joys return
Each time I take a taxi
And their origins I learn.
Back to West Africa
Three times I went last week
And Haiti is a regular
For the broken French I speak.
When English is unusable
And the route from A to B
Is indirect with meter racing
Those pleasant feelings flee.

CARLYN PARKER

The Museum of Natural History, 1931
The New York Times

Les Troyens, Metropolitan Opera House, 2012
Ruby Washington

Upper East Side, 2001

Ruth Fremson

The Dom nightclub, St. Mark's Place, 1966
Larry C. Morris

The Meatpacking District , 1973

Neal Boenzi

Albert S. Pacetta, commissioner of markets, and Nick Apicalla, fruit vendor, Mott and Hester Streets, 1962
Meyer Liebowitz

One World Observatory, 2016
Chang W. Lee

The Highline at Gansevoort Street, 2009
Nicole Bengiveno

Yankees win the World Series, Shea Stadium, 2000
Chang W. Lee

Mets win the World Series, Shea Stadium, 1986
Larry C. Morris

Inspecting propellers of the S.S. *Manhattan*, Brooklyn Naval Yard, 1933
The New York Times

P.S. 1 Contemporary Art Center, Long Island City, 2001
Ruth Fremson

Eli Zabar on The Vinegar Factory rooftop, Upper East Side, 2011
Hiroko Masuike

After Hurricane Sandy, volunteers restore the dunes, Breezy Point, Queens, 2013
Damon Winter

Manhattan-bound on the Brooklyn Bridge, 1979

Neal Boenzi

Brooklyn-bound on the Williamsburg Bridge, 2015
Damon Winter

Chinatown, 2007
Andrea Mohin

East Harlem, 2017
Tony Cenicola

The place was the Little King Restaurant in Bayside, Queens. Barbara Burke, who dined there one recent evening, overheard this much of a conversation between two women seated nearby: "So what do you wear to dim sum?"

Bronx residents cheer Pope John Paul II's motorcade, 1979
Paul Hosefros

Palm Sunday, Church of the Pentecost, Bronx, 2004
Tyler Hicks

New Year in Chinatown, 1975
Neal Boenzi

Good Defeats Evil, United Nations, 2001
Chang W. Lee

Park Avenue and 52nd Street, 2007
Librado Romero

Sheep Meadow, Central Park, 2001
Andrea Mohin

Firefighters in training, Roosevelt Island, 1963

Meyer Liebowitz

Aquashow, Flushing Meadows, Queens, 1951
Sam Falk

Simon O'Neill, Heidi Melton, and John Relyea with the New York Philharmonic,
Jaap van Zweden conducting, David Geffen Hall, Lincoln Center, 2018
Michelle V. Agins

Maya Lahyani, Stephanie Blythe, and Ying Fang in *Cendrillon*,
Metropolitan Opera House, 2018
Sara Krulwich

New York Central freight yards, 72nd Street and 12th Avenue, 1952
Todd Heisler

World Trade Center Transit Hub, Lower Manhattan, 2014

Todd Heisler

Mayoral candidate John V. Lindsay, Far Rockaway, Queens, 1965
Carl T. Gossett Jr.

The Naked Cowboy, Times Square, 2003

Ruth Fremson

Astroland, Coney Island, 1978
Barton Silverman

Tuning up the Thunderbolt, Coney Island, 1954
Neal Boenzi

Grand Central Terminal, 2009
Richard Perry

Grand Central Terminal gleams after a refurbishing, 1998
Fred R. Conrad

It is the morning rush hour. Marion Gutmann of Brooklyn is standing on a subway platform at Grand Central Terminal. A train pulls in; a well-dressed woman gets off. Before the doors close, the woman realizes that she is holding only one of her leather gloves. She looks back in the train and spots the matching one on the seat. It is obviously too late to dash back in to retrieve it. With a cavalier shrug, she flings her arm out and, the doors about to close, tosses her glove onto the seat alongside its mate.

Rangers' Dominic Moore, Madison Square Garden, 2015

Chang W. Lee

Diamond auction, New Yorker Hotel, Manhattan, 2009
G. Paul Burnett

Reindeer Richard, Roosevelt Island Tram, 1977
Chester Higgins Jr.

Limbering up backstage for the Christmas show, Radio City, 2006
Fred R. Conrad

Wall Street parking garage after Hurricane Sandy, 2012
Damon Winter

Pete Correa, a Sandy victim, with the remains of his home, Staten Island, 2012
Chang W. Lee

Pennsylvania Station, Manhattan, 1962
Sam Falk

Pennsylvania Station, Manhattan, 1920
The New York Times

West Side Tennis Club, Forest Hills, Queens, 1969

Carl T. Gossett Jr.

Maria Sharapova serves to Amelie Mauresmo, U.S. Open semifinals, Arthur Ashe Stadium, Queens, 2006
Chang W. Lee

After a monthlong protest, police force students out of Hamilton Hall,
Columbia University, 1968
Larry C. Mørris

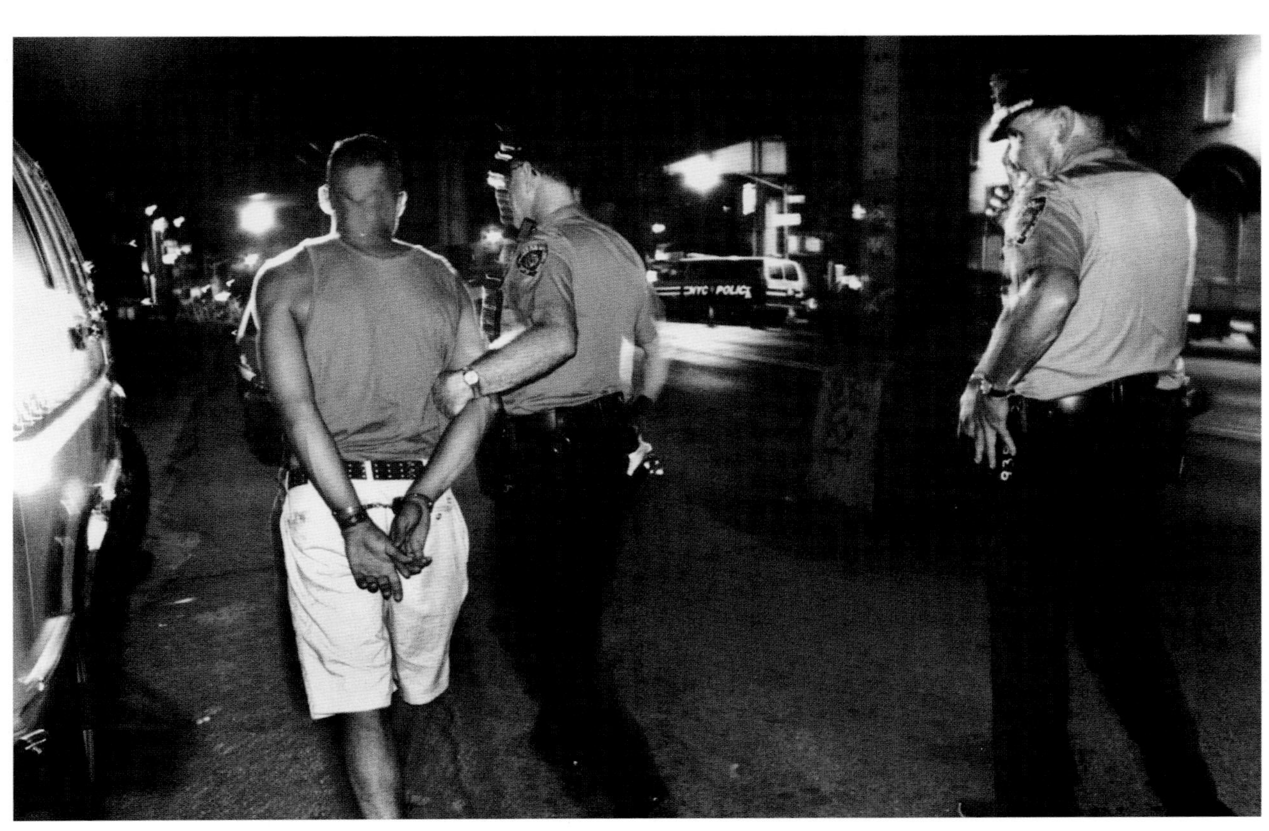

Jerome Avenue and 190th Street, 1994
Monica Almeida

Floor of the New York Stock Exchange during trading, 1987
Jim Wilson

Floor of the New York Stock Exchange after trading, 1951
Patrick A. Burns

Dear Diary:

It's 6:30 P.M. Friday on the M1 bus heading up Madison Avenue. The bus is packed, and a rider, about 30, shoves his way from the back to get off at 61st Street. He gets to the rear door just as the driver locks the doors and is about to pull out. The man lets out an unintelligible scream, causing the other passengers to look around nervously. The bus quickly stops. The driver releases the doors. As the man leaps off, he smiles smugly to another passenger and says softly, "It helps to be a Wall Street Trader."

JEROME C. KATZ

A giraffe from Africa en route to the St. Louis zoo, Pier 1, Brooklyn, 1957
John Orris

Roosevelt Island Tram, stalled by a power outage, Over the East River, 2006

Richard Perry

Indian Independence Day parade, Madison Avenue, Midtown Manhattan, 2009

Damon Winter

Amulya and Alekhya Vppala, Madison Avenue and 25th Street, 2004
Hiroko Masuike

Backyard church service and wedding, Williamsbridge, Bronx, 2008
Todd Heisler

Singer Kat DeLuna during Fashion Week, Bryant Park, 2007
Marilynn K. Yee

Waiting for the S.S. *United States* to arrive, West Side Piers, 1952
Eddie Hausner

The U.S.S. *Constellation* leaves New York for the first time, East River, 1961
Lou Schifano

Teddy at his usual spot, 59th Street and Fifth Avenue, 2014
Damon Winter

Lower Manhattan, 1974
Eddie Hausner

Michael Kors show, Lincoln Center, 2011
Marilynn K. Yee

Long Island City, 2015
Nicole Bengiveno

David Letterman, Ed Sullivan Theater, 2015
Damon Winter

Walter Cronkite, CBS Studios, 1964

Sam Falk

Cross country race, Van Cortland Park, 1956
Eddie Hausner

Wire strung from a building without electricity to one with it,
Eagle Avenue and 161st Street, Bronx, 1973
Neal Boenzi

Woolworth's lunch counter, Manhattan, 1954
Sam Falk

Dekalb Market Hall, Brooklyn, 2017
Hiroko Masuike

Broadway and 43rd Street, 1959
Carl T. Gossett Jr.

Ramp to the Third Avenue Bridge, Bronx, 2013
Angel Franco

Barbara Jusme at her grandmother's window, Nostrand Avenue, Brooklyn, 2004
Tyler Hicks

Columbus Day Parade, Fifth Avenue, 2006
James Estrin

Kendrick Wolf, self-styled "Angelic Janitorial Ramasan,"
42nd Street and Second Avenue, 1976
Paul Hosefros

Fidel Castro aboard the Bronx Zoo train, 1959
Meyer Liebowitz

Dear Diary:

Back in New York after several months in the Midwest, I was leaving the Port Authority terminal when the sound of classical music in the distance stopped me. I found an orchestra of junior high school students performing in their Sunday best. I noticed that beside the splendidly dressed conductor was another raggedly dressed conductor, one who, I suspect, makes his home in the terminal. Side by side, each conductor was thoroughly engrossed in his work and apparently oblivious to the other. "Ah," I said to myself, "home again."

KEN BARON

Grand Street near the Bowery, 2007

Todd Heisler

Aqueduct Racetrack, South Ozone Park, Queens, 1973
Barton Silverman

Midtown Manhattan, from East 57th Street, 1940
The New York Times

The New Year's Eve ball, 1978
Chester Higgins Jr.

Immigration protest, Jackson Heights, Queens, 2006
James Estrin

Danny Moreno, 19, at work, Bronx, 2014
Nicole Bengiveno

Gravesend Park, Brooklyn, 1972
Barton Silverman

Celebrating the Astronauts, Lower Broadway, 1969
Jack Manning

West 58th Street, 2010
Fred R. Conrad

Fifth Avenue, Brooklyn, 2008
Nicole Bengiveno

Dear Diary:

While shopping in the West Village one recent Sunday I stopped to look at a selection of Christmas ornaments and came upon a woman having a very difficult time choosing between two magnificent tree-toppers. She held them up to the light, stared back and forth between the two and said, with great emphasis, "Oy!"

Robin Kappy

125th Street, Harlem, 2008
Nicole Bengiveno

Midtown Manhattan, 2018

Sara Krulwich

Jeffrey's Hook, Fort Washington Park, 2012
Ozier Muhammad

Verrazano-Narrows Bridge, Staten Island, 2009
Todd Heisler

Mike Stone with Rickey, an Alaskan Malamute,
Westminster Kennel Club Show, Madison Square Garden, 2012
Fred R. Conrad

Midtown Manhattan, 2008
Nicole Bengiveno

P.S. 51, West 45th Street, 1975

Neal Boenzi

Brooklyn Technical High School, Fort Greene Place, 2014
Ozier Muhammad

Times Square, 2008
Todd Heisler

West 43rd Street, 2006
Nicole Bengiveno

Veterans Day street fair, Manhattan, 2010
Ruth Fremson

Cambodian Buddhist ceremony, Bronx, 2005
James Estrin

Kate Hudson and Lady Gaga at the Costume Institute Gala, Metropolitan Museum of Art, 2014
Damon Winter

Cookie Monster, Elmo, and less-furry creatures, Times Square, 2014

Damon Winter

West and Cortland Streets, Manhattan, 1960
Allyn Baum

The Woolworth Building, Lower Manhattan, 1950
Arthur Brower

Alicia Keys at Barclays Center, 2013
Richard Perry

Billy Joel at Madison Square Garden, 2012
Damon Winter

Joe Namath, Shea Stadium, 1966
Barton Silverman

NYPD cricket league, Gateway Cricket Grounds, Brooklyn, 2009
Ruby Washington

Immigration ceremony, Ellis Island, 2008
Chang W. Lee

Memorial Day commemoration, Intrepid Sea, Air & Space Museum, Manhattan,
Chang W. Lee

Ocean View Manor, Coney Island, 2001
Nicole Bengiveno

Bronx, 2010
Richard Perry

Gay rights protest, Near City Hall, 1985
Neal Boenzi

Sephanie Spahr-LaFroscia and Theresa LaFroscia, Manhattan Marriage Bureau, 2011
Josh Haner

Overheard by Joel Raphaelson in the East 50's, one young man to another: "Let's go to Tiffany's first and get that over with."

Marking the 50th anniversary of King Kong, 1983
Sara Krulwich

The Rockefeller Center Observation Deck, 1964
Robert Walker

Henrique Prince of The Ebony Hillbillies, Times Square subway station, 2008
Todd Heisler

Leonard Bernstein, Manhattan, 1959
Sam Falk

Sunset Park, Brooklyn, 2007
Todd Heisler

Ram Kissoon and his son Elias, Ferry Point Park, Bronx, 2012
Ruth Fremson

Poetry at The Bizarre coffee shop, Greenwich Village, 1961
Sam Falk

Tools of War Hip Hop Jam, Concrete Park, Bronx, 2014
Todd Heisler

Dear Diary:

Buying a T-shirt at the Pop Shop in SoHo, I asked the cashier what to me was a common question after purchasing an item. "Do you wrap?" The puzzled cashier paused, while I wondered what was so complex about the question. At long last, he replied: "No, but I like listening to it. Why do you ask?"

RICHARD DALTON JR.

141st Street in Harlem, 1957
Robert Walker

61st Street Station, Woodside, Queens, 2008

Richard Perry

Women watching the service for slain Rabbi Chaskel Werzberger, Williamsburg, Brooklyn, 1990
Dith Pran

Funeral for Rabbi Joel Teitelbaum, Williamsburg, Brooklyn, 2006
James Estrin

Ai Weiwei's *Good Fences Make Good Neighbors*, Washington Square Park, 2017
Hiroko Masuike

Fort Tompkins, Staten Island, 2008
Fred R. Conrad

Big Apple Circus, Damrosch Park, Manhattan, 1988
Don Hogan Charles

The Calypso Tumblers, Washington Square Park, 1987
Dith Pran

Lenox Avenue, Harlem, 2006
James Estrin

Yo-Yo Ma and Kathryn Stott, Carnegie Hall, 2010
Chang W. Lee

Trinity Church, Lower Manhattan, 1949

Meyer Liebowitz

A human tower of Catalonians, Fifth Avenue rooftop, 2012
Librado Romero

Brighton Beach, Brooklyn, 1972
Barton Silverman

Nadine Colon buries her cousin Emily Colon in the sand, Coney Island, 2005
Tyler Hicks

The Garment District, West 36th Street, 1967
Arthur Brower

West 58th Street, 1975
Eddie Hausner

Overheard in the lobby of an apartment building in the East 70s:
Concierge to doorman: **"20B wants to know if it's a fur coat or cloth coat day."**
Doorman to concierge: **"For me it's always cloth."**

In formation over Midtown Manhattan, 1947
Meyer Liebowitz

Empire State Building struck by a B-25, 1945
Ernie Sisto

The Pioneers vs. The Jolters, Shea Stadium, 1973
Michael Evans

Sister Mary Elizabeth and Sister Immaculata, West Side Highway path, 2006
Tyler Hicks

Fifth Avenue and 57th Street, 2013
Ozier Muhammad

Michael and Ann Zhang, Central Park, 2005

Vincent Laforet

The Christian Cultural Center, Flatlands Avenue, Brooklyn, 2009
Todd Heisler

Elaine Stritch at The Carlyle, Upper East Side, 2013
Todd Heisler

42nd Street near Park Avenue, 2010
Damon Winter

Eight-vehicle collision, Seventh Avenue and 52nd Street, date unknown
Patrick A. Burns

Sri Lankans have a pillow fight, Henry Kaufmann Campgrounds, Staten Island, 2013

James Estrin

Watching Bolivia vs. Colombia in the World Cup, Café España, Queens, 2007
Todd Heisler

Upper West Side, 2003
Vincent Laforet

Under the Manhattan Bridge, 2010

Todd Heisler

Jiggs the chimpanzee at a Police Athletic League benefit, Tavern on the Green, 1986
Chester Higgins Jr.

Bush Terminal, Brooklyn, 1957
John Orris

On a recent rainy Sunday, Susan Cohen and a friend took their children to the Museum of Natural History. They traveled up and down the crowded elevators and stairs, saw the barosaurus and elephants, dioramas of wetland birds, desert animals and cactuses, an Indian wedding and scenes from Antarctica. They ate lunch in the dark under the whale. Everyone was getting tired. But five-year-old Rebecca had had it. She kept begging to be taken to the "fun floor" but was unable or unwilling to describe what she meant. Wherever she went, it wasn't the fun floor. Finally, in exasperation, she exclaimed, "I'm tired of looking at boring interesting stuff."

Croton Water Filtration Plant, Bronx, 2011

Fred R. Conrad

Ground Zero, five years after, 2006
Vincent Laforet

South Street Seaport, Manhattan, 2008
Nicole Bengiveno

Circle Line tours, West Side Piers, 2015
Todd Heisler

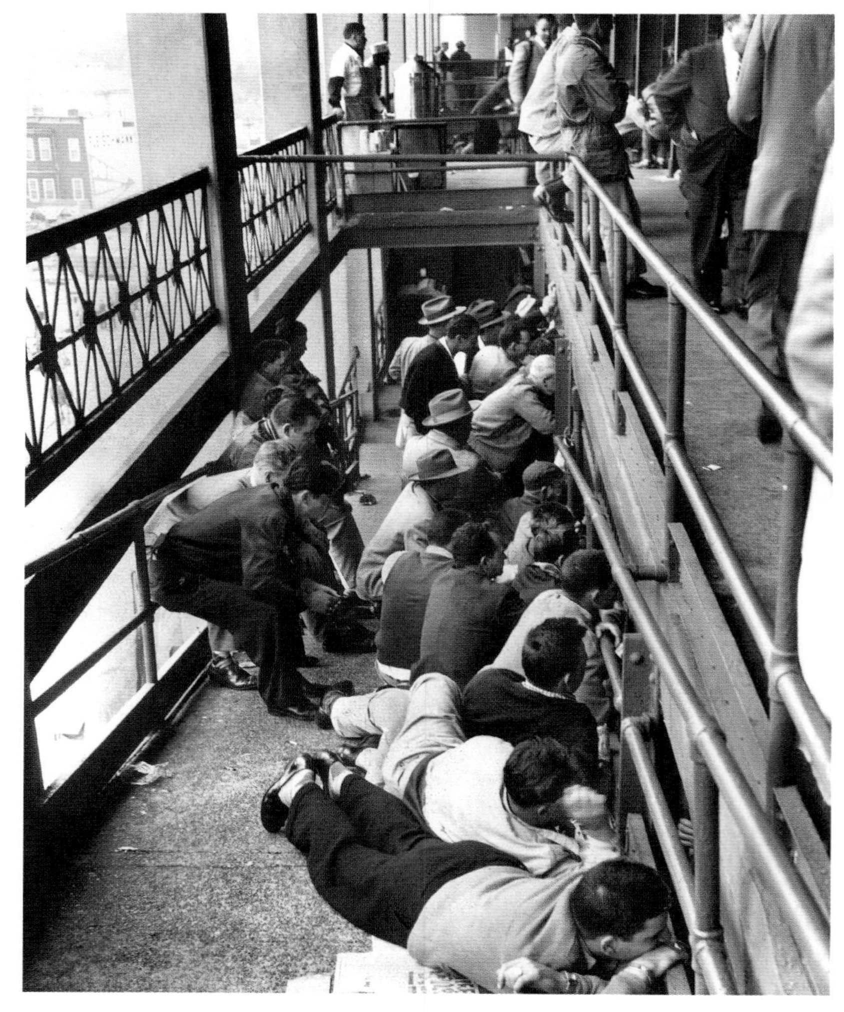

Dodgers vs. Yankees in the World Series, Ebbets Field, 1955

Carl T. Gossett Jr.

Yankees vs. Dodgers in the World Series, Yankee Stadium, 1947
Sam Falk

Roberta Peters prepares for *Don Pasquale*, Eaves Costumer, 46th Street, 1955
Sam Falk

Isaac Mizrahi show, Bryant Park, 2009
Todd Heisler

From the observation deck, 70 Pine Street, Lower Manhattan, 2012

James Estrin

Gowanus Canal, Brooklyn, 1971
Meyer Liebowitz

The Dead Boys at CBGB, Bowery and Bleecker Streets, 1977
Fred R. Conrad

Maya Angelou and Amiri Baraka, Schomburg Library, Malcolm X Boulevard, 1991
Chester Higgins, Jr.

Washington Mews, Greenwich Village, 2017
Hiroko Masuike

The Highline at West 23rd Street, Manhattan, 2015
Hiroko Masuike

Dear Diary:

Overheard on the subway, a conversation between two 20-something women:

First woman: **"I'm going to his loft in SoHo tonight. He says it's big—4,000 square feet."**

Second woman: **"Wow—4,000 square feet is huge!"**

First woman: **"I don't know. I think it probably just has really high ceilings."**

Second woman: **"Yeah. You're probably right."**

JAY SULLIVAN

Metrocard machines, 42nd Street subway station, 2015

Ruth Fremson

Track work at Penn Station, 2017
Hiroko Masuike

Martin Luther King Jr. in Queens, a week before his assassination,
Northern Boulevard, Corona, 1968
John Orris

Congress of Racial Equality demonstration, Manhattan, 1965
Jack Manning

Cycles of Expression exhibition, Grand Central Terminal, 1995
Ruby Washington

Mercer and Spring Streets, SoHo, 2013

Damon Winter

Veterans Day Parade, Fifth Avenue, 2013
Ozier Muhammad

Puerto Rican Day Parade, Fifth Avenue, 2006
Michelle V. Agins

Helen Hayes Theater, West 44th Street, 2001

Fred R. Conrad

Pennsylvania Station, 1966
Sam Falk

Nick Young and Christine Ko have their engagement photo taken,
Broadway and Morris Street, 2008
Todd Heisler

Fifth Avenue and 60th Street, 1971
Don Hogan Charles

Dear Diary:

I was on a crowded 96th Street crosstown bus early one recent evening when several passengers got on at the Fifth Avenue stop, including a couple carrying several large framed pictures in bubble wrap. As the bus was about to cross the park, the male half of the couple reached into a bag he was also carrying and pulled out a small blue Tiffany box, tied with white ribbon. The woman had a giant smile on her face—at first I thought they had bought whatever was in the box together, but the young man handed the little package to his companion and she began opening it expectantly. Nestled on velvet was a diamond ring, and it went right on her finger. The two were smiling as they gazed into each other's eyes. "We met on this bus," the woman explained to her fellow passengers. Taken with the moment, all the other riders applauded.

SHELLEY ANN HAINER

Gotham Scooter Rally, Madison Avenue, 2005
Richard Perry

Michael Volle and Anna Netrebko in *Tosca*, Metropolitan Opera House, 2018
Sara Krulwich

Charles Ponte with a customer at his music store,
West 54th Street, where such stores once flourished, 1968
Patrick A. Burns

Blowing cool in the cold, Lee Goodson on Fifth Avenue and 54th Street, 2013
Ruth Fremson

World Seido Karate Organization, Rockaway Beach, Queens, 1999
Librado Romero

Dance of the Monkey, Flower Drum Restaurant, Manhattan, 1980
Chester Higgins Jr.

Michael Lechrichia walks Vito Vincent, East River Park, 2013
Todd Heisler

Preparing for a Mardi Gras ball, Sheraton Astor Hotel, 1956
Meyer Liebowitz

The Taking of Pelham One Two Three on location, Brooklyn, 1974
Larry C. Morris

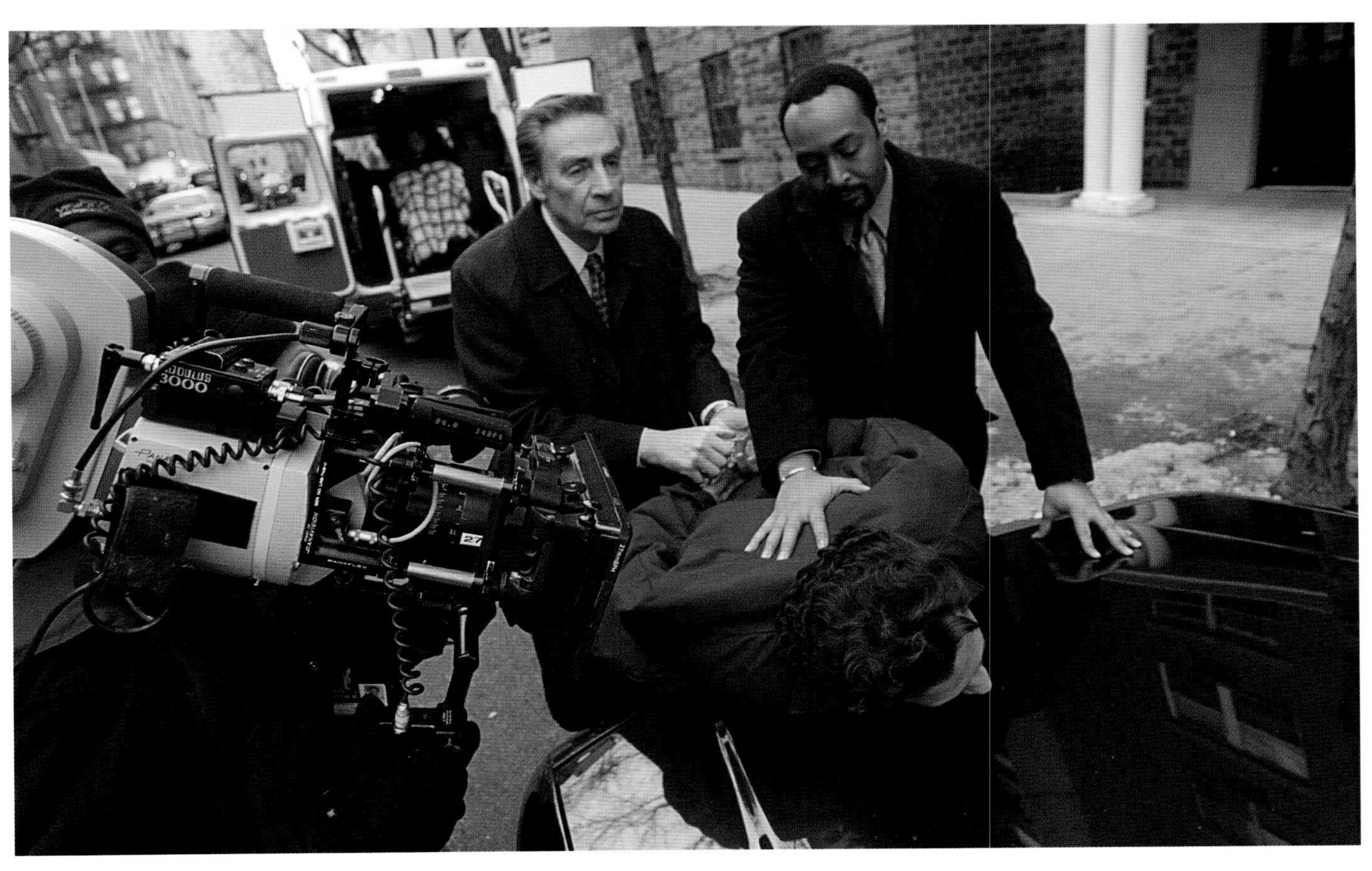

Jerry Orbach and Jesse L. Martin shooting *Law and Order*, West 54th Street, 2004
Librado Romero

Met Opera Orchestra members pack their instruments, 39th Street and Broadway, 1942
Sam Falk

Carnegie Hall stage, Seventh Avenue and 57th Street, 1990
Fred R. Conrad

Johnny Marx on the keyboards, Madison Square Park, 2014
Chang W. Lee

Taking a break from reading in Bryant Park, 2009
Todd Heisler

A MANHATTAN MOMENT

I can tell you
that the yellow turned
to red and I stepped
off the curb
and a car passed inches
from my front shoe.
So bullet-fast.
I can't tell you
about panic
or rage, sorrow
or regret.
All I felt
a minute later
was open-mouthed
amazement,
to be already
thinking about
what to have
for lunch.

Robert K. Johnson

High Line, Manhattan, 2007
Damon Winter

Paul Rosen snaps and Billy poses, Manhattan, 1963
John Orris

Liselotte Waldheim and Carl Ritter von Rohrer,
Practicing for the Viennese Opera Ball, Fifth Avenue, 1966
Jack Manning

Debutante Ball, Waldorf Astoria, 1968

Larry C. Morris

Sakura Matsuri Festival, Brooklyn Botanic Garden, 2012
Fred R. Conrad

Jazzbo waits for the Rockaway express, Times Square, 1958
Allyn Baum

Boardwalk, Coney Island, 1975
Eddie Hausner

Gary Atlas, Brighton Beach, Brooklyn, 2018
Todd Heisler

Broadway Central Hotel after its collapse, Broadway near Houston Street, 1973
Meyer Liebowitz

United Airlines plane wreckage following a midair collision, Park Slope, Brooklyn, 1960
Ernie Sisto

Boys Choir of Harlem and the Vienna Boys Choir, Great Hall, City College, 2002
Suzanne DeChillo

Justice Sonia Sotomayor and the Cardinal Spellman High School band,
Sonia Sotomayor Houses, Bronx, 2010
Todd Heisler

The Playpen peep show, Eighth Avenue, 2014
Richard Perry

New Year's party, Times Square, 2002
Richard Perry

They used to call it Hell's Kitchen,
But now that it's starting to cook,
(And gaining in fame)
They'll be changing its name
And calling it Hell's Breakfast Nook.
MICHAEL WINSHIP

Hong Kong Dragon Boats, Flushing Meadows, Queens, 2010

Suzanne DeChillo

Chinese New Year parade, Mott Street, 2014
Damon Winter

Adam Clayton Powell Jr. and followers, Seventh Avenue, Harlem, 1968

Don Hogan Charles

Rev. Wyatt T. Walker speaks to parishioners, 116th Street, Harlem, 1970
Michael Evans

The Oak Room, Plaza Hotel, 1974

Paul Hosefros

Plaza Hotel, Fifth Avenue and 60th Street, 2011
Ruth Fremson

Prepping for the "Grand National" stock car race, Polo Grounds, 1959
Ernie Sisto

Oak Point Avenue, Bronx, 2003
Joyce Dopkeen

Bull rider Jack Sogen, Weissglass Stadium, Staten Island, 1970
Barton Silverman

Union Square Park, 2009
Damon Winter

In the Catacombs of the Metropolitan Museum of Art , 1946
The New York Times

Jonathan Cohen, aka Meres One, Five Pointz, Long Island City, 2015
Todd Heisler

Victor Sala, banquet waiter, Waldorf Astoria, Park Avenue, 2015
Todd Heisler

McSorley's Old Ale House, East Seventh Street, 1966
Sam Falk

Times Square, 1953
Neal Boenzi

Fresh Kills landfill, Staten Island, 1972
William E. Sauro

Whitney Museum of American Art, Gansevoort Street, 2015
Damon Winter

Hamilton Heights, Manhattan, 2001
Chang W. Lee

THE AVENUE DESERTED

Roller-
skating in the rain, the best
of fellows in the worst of times,
he has a butterfly chic in his elbows.
Such dissection of a puddle is pure dash.
The water leaps up behind him
with the obedience that usually
follows a taxi.
It really looks like something
More than love, or the late, wet hour
That makes him lurch so beautifully
Down the street -
He doesn't look banished or even damp.
This must be his profession.

C.L. KEYWORTH

Meatpacking District, Manhattan, 1970s
Carl T. Gossett Jr.

Gold Street, Lower Manhattan, 2006
Tyler Hicks

Antiwar demonstration, First Avenue near the United Nations, 2003
Suzanne DeChillo

Theater District, 1999

Richard Perry

Harlem, 2000
Chang W. Lee

Harlem, 2013
Ozier Muhammad

Fifth Avenue and 101st Street, 2010

Ruth Fremson

Times Square, 2004
Don Hogan Charles

Comic Con, Javits Center, Manhattan, 2014
Fred R. Conrad

Truman Capote at the Black and White Ball, Plaza Hotel, 1966
Barton Silverman

Ninth Avenue and 28th Street, 2003

James Estrin

Church of the Holy Apostles, Ninth Avenue near 29th Street, 2015

Todd Heisler

Alto saxophonist Micah Gaugh, Café Khufu, East Village, 2010
Ozier Muhammad

Astoria Generating Station, Queens, 2012
Ruth Fremson

Coty Awards Show, Metropolitan Museum of Art, 1966
Robert Walker

Sugar Ray Robinson, 123rd Street, Harlem, 1951
Sam Falk

Gus the polar bear, Central Park Zoo, 2011
Hiroko Masuike

Hamilton Fish Pool, East Village, 1992
Angel Franco

Olive is rescued, Broadway near West Third Street, 1973
Neal Boenzi

A scorched building in which two firefighters died, East 178th Street, Bronx, 2005
Vincent Laforet

Chef Roger Fessaguet, La Caravelle restaurant, West 55th Street, 1962
Sam Falk

Food cart in the Wall Street area, 2008
Nicole Bengiveno

Sign, spotted by Edwin Kennebeck, in the window of the C & S Pizza Parlor on Eighth Avenue: NO FOOD OR DRINK ALLOWED IN STORE

Paul Simon and Art Garfunkel, Palladium, East 14th Street, 1981
Fred R. Conrad

The Beatles arrive, John F. Kennedy International Airport, Queens, 1964
Carl T. Gossett Jr.

The USS *Constellation,* Brooklyn Naval Yard, 1957
Neal Boenzi

Hudson Yards redevelopment, Manhattan, 2016
Chang W. Lee

Millennium celebration, Times Square, 2000
Nicole Bengiveno

Spike Lee roots for the Knicks, Madison Square Garden, 2009
Barton Silverman

Brooklyn Boulders climbing gym, Gowanus, Brooklyn, 2014
Damon Winter

The Garment District, Manhattan, 2013

Hiroko Masuike

Watching election results in Times Square, 1944

Ernie Sisto

Checking on the stock market, Broad Street, Manhattan, 1968

William E. Sauro

Diane von Furstenberg, Manhattan, 2009

Todd Heisler

At the Tory Burch fall show, Alice Tully Hall, Lincoln Center, 2012
Marilynn K. Yee

Roosevelt Avenue, Queens, 2008
Richard Perry

42nd Street, Manhattan, 2018
Todd Heisler

"Several weeks ago," writes Ethel Davis, "I was racing down West End Avenue toward 66th Street to catch the bus that was approaching that corner. As I got on the bus, the driver looked at me and said, 'I don't know why you're getting on this bus for, lady. You're making much better time than I am.'"

Sneaking a preview of the circus, Eighth Avenue and 50th Street, 1946
Ernie Sisto

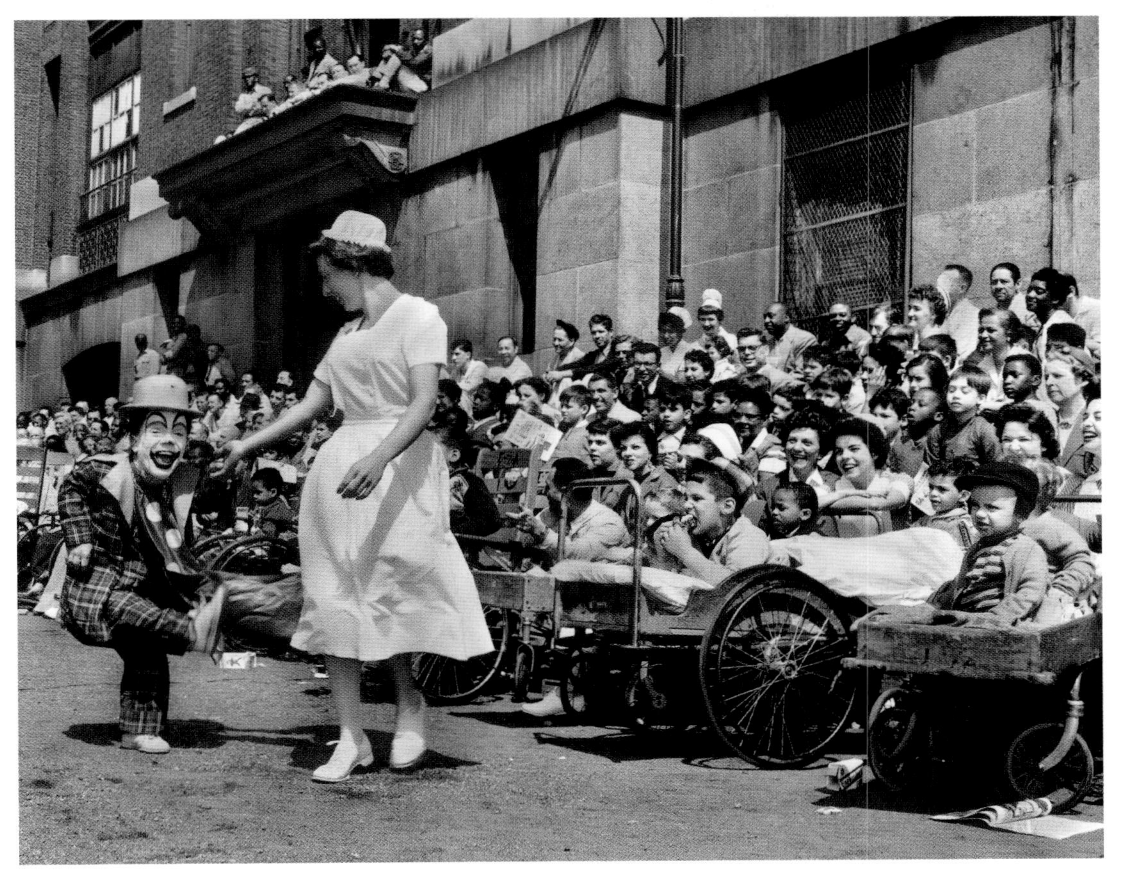

Jimmy Armstrong the clown with Nurse Anneliese Zassoda,
Bellevue Hospital, Manhattan, 1955
Fred Sass

Power-wash day, East 62nd Street, Manhattan, 2005
Ruth Fremson

Near Erie Basin Park, Brooklyn, 2010
Nicole Bengiveno

Queen Elizabeth, United Nations General Assembly, 2010
Todd Heisler

The Queen and the Duke of Edinburgh, Broadway, 1976
Tyrone Dukes

Ninth Avenue and 41st Street, Manhattan, 2016
Richard Perry

Segundo Minchala hangs Christmas lights, Queens, 2007
Todd Heisler

Nino D'Eramo checks the Grand Central Terminal clock, Date unknown
Keith Meyers

Cleaning the lobby chandelier, Metropolitan Opera House, 1981
Jack Manning

The scene is the lobby of the New York State Theater during the first intermission of a recent *La Bohème*. One woman to another, overheard by Joe Morrone: "All the doctors seem younger these days, and the police officers, too." Pause. "And now the opera singers!"

Jerry Seinfeld, 79th Street and Broadway, 2002
Chester Higgins Jr.

Al Sharpton, NBC Studios, 2003
Fred R. Conrad

El Parador, Manhattan, 1966

Larry C. Morris

St. Regis Hotel roof, Fifth Avenue, 1968

Larry C. Morris

Dismantling the Gimbels-Saks connector, Above 33rd Street, Manhattan, 1966

Robert Walker

Central Synagogue after it was badly damaged by a fire, Midtown Manhattan, 1998
Suzanne DeChillo

In a Chinatown store, Manhattan, 2010

Marcus Yam

Viva, Andy Warhol, and Ultra Violet, Location unknown, 1968
Sam Falk

Tour bus driver, Fifth Avenue in Midtown Manhattan, 2008
Nicole Bengiveno

Manhattan, 2008
Nicole Bengiveno

Eighth Avenue and 42nd Street, Manhattan, 1957
Eddie Hausner

Eighth Avenue and 40th Street, Manhattan, 1970
Patrick A. Burns

Standing on the corner of Avenue of the Americas and Minetta Lane after a theater performance recently, Jimmy Nicholas, a New York printing executive, flagged a taxi to take his wife and a friend to dinner. As the taxi approached, so did a giant waterbug, that scourge of New York summers. As the women watched in horror, the bug veered from a puddle and scurried toward the door of the taxi. Mr. Nicholas squashed it.
"I had to," he told the crowd at the corner, which burst into applause.
"It was trying to steal our cab."

Madison Square Garden, 2004
Vincent Laforet

Lower Manhattan, 2013
Librado Romero

The steps at TKTS, Times Square, 2011
Damon Winter

Mott and Mosco Streets, Manhattan, 2016
Hiroko Matsui

Metro North waiting room, Grand Central Terminal, 2006
Nicole Bengiveno

Prospect Park Tennis Center, Brooklyn, 2011

Nicole Bengiveno

Manhattan, 2009
Librado Romero

Lower Manhattan, 2009

Damon Winter

Fifth Avenue, Manhattan, 2008
Nicole Bengiveno

Rockefeller Center, 2006

Fred R. Conrad

Matt Cruz, Lower East Side, 2016
Hiroko Masuike

Breezy Point Surf Club, Queens, 2000
Nicole Bengiveno

Harpist Carol Baum makes a shoe change, Park Avenue, 1955

Fred Sass

Benny Goodman and the New Music String Quartet, Bryant Park, 1952
Meyer Liebowitz

President John F. Kennedy with Mayor Robert Wagner, Midtown Manhattan, 1961
Carl T. Gossett Jr.

Mayoral candidate Bill de Blasio on the stump, Jamaica, Queens, 2013
Damon Winter

Rock climbers assembling an art installation,
Metropolitan Museum of Art roof garden, 2010
Librado Romero

Oliver and Henry Streets, 1974
Neal Boenzi

Midtown Manhattan, 1973
Don Hogan Charles

Empire State Building, 2008
Nicole Bengiveno

Fort Tryon Park, Manhattan, 1991

Angel Franco

Johanna Krauss, Inwood Hill Park, Manhattan, 1997
Suzanne DeChillo

Spanish Harlem, 1964
Sam Falk

Washington Square art bazaar, 1963
Sam Falk

Watching the second of two uninvited climbers scale
The New York Times Building, West Side, Manhattan, 2008
Ruby Washington

The first climber, Alain Robert, aka Spiderman, is met by a policeman at the top, 2008
David Scull

Monk parrots and their nest, Howard Beach, Queens, 2014
Angel Franco

Spires of St. Patrick's, seen through the sphere of Atlas, Midtown Manhattan, 2010
Ruth Fremson

Weary traveler, Pennsylvania Station, 1955
Larry C. Morris

Ray Cannavaro writes finis to a beloved movie palace, Flatbush Avenue, Brooklyn, 1964
Patrick A. Burns

Profound thanks for this book go first and foremost to those whose work is on display in its pages. They are, or were, staff photographers for *The New York Times*, a publication long referred to as The Gray Lady, which, translated, meant 'not particularly visual.' That label has happily disappeared, but this book is a vivid reminder that our photographers were always a talented bunch. So extraordinary were their efforts, in fact, that it took those of us involved several more years than expected to assemble this collection. Part of the reason was the sheer wealth of wonderful material, and part was dealing with an enormous archive of negatives and prints that was undergoing the process of digitization.

The list of those responsible for assembling what you are now holding begins with Vin Alabiso, who initiated the early research, and ends with Darcy Eveleigh, an indispensable asset to any venture into *The Times* photo archive, who skillfully and tirelessly saw it to completion. David W. Dunlap, the paper's informal historian (and institution), provided sage advice and good humor. Other helpful *Times*folk were archivist Jeffrey P. Roth and William P. O'Donnell in the photo lab. Joseph Han, Alex Klein, Andy Liang and the remarkably creative design team at Pentagram endured our daily whims to create a striking volume, and Charles Miers and James Muschett at Rizzoli lent excellent suggestions and patient support.

In the interest of full disclosure, two items: Though this book advertises itself as a visual Valentine to the crowded, maddening, friendly, crazy, funny, scary, sleep-deprived five-borough agglomeration we are so fond of, there is one photo that was taken beyond the city limits. (Clue: it's on Page 119 and the location is Connecticut, probably near Stamford.) And though the subtitle promises 500 moments, there are actually 502. But who's counting?

Alex Ward

The Photographers

Michelle V. Agins
Monica Almeida
Allyn Baum
Nicole Bengiveno
Neal Boenzi
Arthur Brower
G. Paul Burnett
Patrick A. Burns
Tony Cenicola
Don Hogan Charles
Fred R. Conrad
Suzanne DeChillo
Joyce Dopkeen
Tyrone Dukes
William C. Eckenberg
James Estrin
Michael Evans
Sam Falk
Angel Franco
Ruth Fremson
D. Gorton
Carl T. Gossett Jr.
Josh Haner
Eddie Hausner
Todd Heisler
Tyler Hicks
Chester Higgins Jr.
Paul Hosefros
Edward Keating
Sara Krulwich
Vincent Laforet
Chang W. Lee
Jack Manning
Meyer Liebowitz
Jack Manning
Hiroko Masuike
Keith Meyers
Andrea Mohin
Larry C. Morris
Ozier Muhammad
Dan Neville
John Orris
Richard Perry
Dith Pran
Librado Romero
Fred Sass
William E. Sauro
Lou Schifano
David Scull
Barton Silverman
Ernie Sisto
John Sotomayor
Robert Walker
Ruby Washington
Earl Wilson
Jim Wilson
Damon Winter
Marcus Yam
Marilynn K. Yee

Published by Universe Publishing, a division of
Rizzoli International Publications, Inc.
300 Park Avenue South
New York, New York 10010
www.rizzoliusa.com

Quotes in this book originally appeared in The Metropolitan Diary feature of *The New York Times*.

The New York Times
Editor: Alex Ward
Photo Editor: Darcy Eveleigh

Design by Pentagram
Natasha Jen, Joseph Han, Maurann Stein, Boqin Peng, Karming Wong, Ena Yun, Andy Liang, Jisoo Eom, Sammie Purulak, Veronica Höglund, Alex Klein

2019 2020 2021 2022 / 10 9 8 7 6 5 4 3 2 1

Printed in China

ISBN-13: 978-0-7893-3655-2
Library of Congress Control Number: 2018963149